A Nation Mourns: Bishop James Madison's Memorial Eulogy on The Death of George Washington

Delivered
February 22, 1800
in Bruton Parish Church,
Williamsburg, Virginia

Edited and with Introductory Essays by David L. Holmes
College of William & Mary

Foreword by The Rev. Billy Graham

Introduction by James C. Rees, Executive Director
Mount Vernon Ladies' Association

The Mount Vernon Ladies' Association
Mount Vernon, Virginia
©1999 by The Mount Vernon Ladies' Association
All rights reserved. Published 1999.
ISBN 0-931917-32-8

This publication has been made possible by
the following generous donors:

Mr. L. Keith Mullins

The College of William & Mary

The Friends of Historic Christ Church, Alexandria

Mr. and Mrs. W. Temple Webber, Jr.
In Memory of Commander Charles A. Whiteford

The Parke Rouse Virginia History Fund
City of Williamsburg 300th Anniversary Commission

TABLE OF CONTENTS

George Washington, by Charles Willson Peale, c. 1795.

FOREWORD

No individual contributed more to the founding of the American nation than George Washington—patriot, general, president, first citizen. Unquestionably our nation's history would have been vastly different without his wisdom and leadership.

Two centuries have not dimmed his greatness, and yet his story needs to be retold to each generation—not just to refresh our memories, but to remind us again of the principles on which our forefathers built this nation, and which have made it great. In this reprint of Bishop James Madison's stirring eulogy of our first president—delivered originally in Williamsburg in 1800, and soon widely circulated across the nation—we see anew the high esteem with which Washington was held by his contemporaries.

But through Bishop Madison's eloquent words we also see the spiritual and moral principles which undergirded George Washington's life. He was a man who believed profoundly in God, and in the need to seek His guidance through the Bible and through prayer. He also knew that any nation which ignored God and His moral laws could not long survive in peace—a lesson which is just as relevant now as it was 200 years ago.

Bishop Madison's words spoken in 1800 still speak to us today: "...in an age when even our relation to a God has been derided by wickedness and folly;...bear in mind the example of Washington...O! make that God your friend."

May the lesson of George Washington's life continue to inspire and challenge us for generations to come.

Billy Graham

Bishop James Madison, courtesy Virginia Historical Society, Richmond, VA.

INTRODUCTION

A few weeks after George Washington's death, Abigail Adams wrote of him that "Simple Truth is his best his greatest Eulogy. She alone can render his Fame immortal." Nevertheless, hundreds of eulogies poured forth, as church ministers, civic leaders and others expressed the grief of their communities. Overseas, Napoleon Bonaparte delivered an oration on Washington's virtues and the British Royal Navy lowered its battle ensigns in tribute. At home in America, citizens mourned as for a father. Throughout the sixteen states and in the frontier settlements of the western territories, mock funeral processions filled the streets, men and women dressed in black, and orators delivered eulogies on village greens, from church pulpits, and in town halls. The American people entered the new century joined together in universal mourning.

On February 22, 1800, in Bruton Parish Church in Williamsburg, the Reverend James Madison delivered a eulogy that was soon regarded as the most perfect tribute to Washington's life and legacy. Printers seized upon Bishop Madison's words and his oration remained in print, undergoing many editions, for over forty years.

An intriguing aspect of Madison's eulogy is that it reflects the assessment of a knowledgeable contemporary on the importance of religion in Washington's life. Although Madison was a leader in the Episcopal Church, this did not automatically slant his view of Washington's spirituality. The Revolutionary concepts that Washington championed had, in fact, been ruinous to the Episcopal Church, depriving it of its government-mandated congregations, tithes, and prestige by enacting the separation of church and state. The years after the Revolution impoverished most Episcopal churches in Virginia, yet Madison's words show unaffected admiration for Washington and unshakeable confidence in his faith and devotion.

One of the most comprehensive collections of original Washington eulogies is to be found today in the library at

Mount Vernon. Donated to the Mount Vernon Ladies' Association in 1952, it was a gift of the noted antiquarian John W. Jackson, who spent years assembling the nearly seven hundred titles, many of them items of great rarity. The Jackson Collection includes both American and foreign imprints, most of them first editions of eulogies delivered and printed in the year 1800. The Collection also shows that February 22, Washington's birthday, had already become the day that America would remember him. A great many of the eulogies, like Bishop Madison's, were delivered on that date, formalizing a tradition that had begun at Valley Forge in the winter of 1778.

In life George Washington had achieved an unquestioned pre-eminence in the most extraordinary generation of statesmen this country has ever produced. For the American people, yearning for a new national mythology, Washington embodied the best hopes and the most glorious chapters of their brief history. His image had supplanted that of the repudiated king as the symbolic personification of the nation. His death was a coming of age for the country.

As Americans united in mourning his loss, they celebrated both their common nationhood and the shining destiny Washington had envisioned for a free and united people whose lands would stretch to the unmapped shores of the Pacific.

James C. Rees
Executive Director
Mount Vernon Ladies' Association

A Nation Mourns: Bishop James Madison's Memorial Eulogy on The Death of George Washington

O N THURsday, December 12, 1799, in the sixty-seventh year of his age and in the third year of his retirement from the presidency of the United States, George Washington made his usual long inspection rounds of his Mount Vernon estate on horseback. It was a day on which snow and sleet alternated with rain. By Friday, December 13, a day on which he also left the mansion to ride briefly, Washington had developed a sore throat. Retiring around 9 p.m. on the evening of December 13, the former president rejected his secretary's suggestion that he take medication, declaring that he always preferred to let a cold "go as it came."

Finding himself suffocating and barely able to speak at some point between 2 a.m. and 3 a.m. on December 14, Washington awakened his wife Martha, but refused to allow her to send for aid until dawn. Throughout the following day, Washington's secretary, his overseer, and three conscientious physicians—

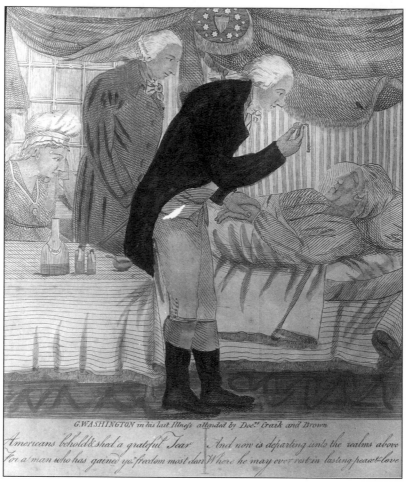

G. Washington in his last hours, c. 1800.

"governed," as one of the latter accurately wrote, "by the best light we had"—attended him. In one of the best known examples of eighteenth-century medicine, the treatment included venesection, or "bleeding." In the years since, medical writers have variously diagnosed Washington's illness as tonsillitis, pneumonia, angina, tuberculosis, cancer, diphtheria, acute laryngitis, and especially a virulent streptococcic infection of the throat. Whatever its nature, all treatments, including a final one of producing blisters on the legs and applying poultices to the throat, failed.

As December 14 progressed, Washington markedly weakened. Martha sat by the bed, his servant stood nearby, his friend and physician James Craik stared helplessly into the fire, the other physicians waited downstairs, and a group of house servants stood anxiously by the bedroom door. Delivering his will to Martha, Washington instructed his secretary about his papers and burial wishes. After sitting for a last time in a chair near his bed, uttering his last words of " 'Tis well," and taking his own pulse, he died peacefully in his bed a little after 10 p.m. on the night of Saturday, December 14, 1799. Four days later, following Episcopal and Masonic services, Washington's family and friends buried him in the old family vault at Mount Vernon within sound of the Potomac River.

Since George Washington had not only led America's armies to independence but also served as its first president, his death occasioned the greatest grief yet known to the new republic. "The whole United States," a Signer of the Declaration of Independence noted, "mourned for him as a father." In the capital at Philadelphia, Congress learned of his death on the morning of December 18 from a passenger on a stage. Immediately adjourning, it reconvened the next day to adopt resolutions and to establish a period of national mourning.

In keeping with a Congressional resolution, President John Adams proclaimed the following February 22 (the anniversary of Washington's birth, which Americans had celebrated unofficially since the 1780s) as the official national day of mourning. Legislatures, city councils, and town meetings quickly followed with similar resolutions. Black suits, black dresses, black sleevebands, and other black ornamentation marked the period of mourning. In Philadelphia Congress wore mourning garb; a black shroud covered the chair of the speaker of the House. Throughout the United States, thousands of citizens—including First Lady Abigail Adams and the entire Regular Army— wore the formal trappings of mourning for months after February 22. In Williamsburg, Virginia, the president of the College of William and Mary, Bishop James Madison, dressed in mourning garb and asked the students of William and Mary to wear pieces of black crape.

13

Solemn eulogies and memorial sermons marked the official period of mourning. From the last days of December, 1799, through February 22, 1800, in almost 200 towns from Castine, Maine, to Natchez, Mississippi, specially selected orators delivered a known total of more than 300 discourses in memory of Washington.

More than half of the orations were delivered on the official day of mourning of February 22, 1800. In New Haven, President Timothy Dwight of Yale spoke; in New Brunswick, New Jersey, Major General Frederick Frelinghuysen; in Philadelphia, Major William Jackson, one of Washington's aides-de-camp; in Baltimore, Roman Catholic Bishop John Carroll; in Alexandria, Dr. Elisha C. Dick, one of the physicians present at Washington's deathbed; in Charleston, South Carolina, the influential Baptist minister Richard Furman. Legislatures, churches, town councils, citizens' committees, Masonic lodges, patriotic societies, and newspapers sponsored or printed most of the orations. From one discourse delivered in Philadelphia twelve days after Washington's death came the well-known description of him as "first in war, first in peace, first in the hearts of his countrymen." From another, scholars once thought, came the fictitious story of young George Washington and the cherry tree.

For the citizens of Williamsburg, Virginia, the memorial address was especially meaningful. Virginia's colonial capital ranked behind only Alexandria and Philadelphia in its historical associations with Washington. Williamsburg had provided the setting for Washington's sixteen years of service in the House of Burgesses, for his many appearances both on personal and on family business before the General Court, for the linking of the American and French armies prior to the Battle of Yorktown, and for much of his pre-Revolutionary socializing and shopping. As a young man of seventeen, he had received his surveyor's license from Williamsburg's College of William and Mary; at the time of his death, he was serving as William and Mary's chancellor. As an Episcopalian, he had frequently worshipped in Williamsburg's Bruton Parish Church. He had close friends in the old capital. Hence it was appropriate that the citizen selected to deliver the memorial oration in Williamsburg on the national day of mourning was both the president of William and Mary and the Episcopal Bishop of Virginia. He was also a man whom President John Tyler, a William and Mary graduate, described as one of the most eloquent speakers he had ever heard.

Born in 1749 in the Shenandoah Valley of Virginia, Bishop James Madison (1749-1812) graduated with highest honors from William and Mary in 1772. Although he studied law under the famous George Wythe, he joined the William and Mary faculty in 1773 as professor of mathematics. Travelling to England two years later for ordination to the Anglican ministry, he returned to find William and Mary torn by the tensions of the Revolutionary War. In 1777 he was elected president in place of the Reverend John Camm, a Tory who returned to England rather than swear allegiance to the American Revolution.

An earnest patriot during the Revolution, Madison served as captain of William and Mary's company of militia. Always

Silhouette, Bishop James Madison.

15

interested in national affairs, he allied himself after the war with the emerging Republican-Democratic forces led by his second cousin James Madison, by his friend and frequent correspondent Thomas Jefferson, and by his former student James Monroe. During the thirty-six years of Bishop Madison's presidency, no other college in America produced as many national leaders as William and Mary. Elected first Bishop of Virginia in 1790, Madison served simultaneously as president of William and Mary, as one of its professors, and (until 1802) as rector of James City Parish, the oldest Episcopal parish in America.

As his record of activities indicates, Bishop Madison was clearly one of the gifted men of eighteenth-century America. Described by his cousin President James Madison as "particularly distinguished by a candour, a benevolence, a politeness of mind, and a courtesy of manner that won the confidence and affection on the shortest acquaintance," he was the friend and correspondent not only of Jefferson and Monroe but also of men such as Edmund Randolph, Benjamin Rush, Joel Barlow, and William Wirt. One of the leading American scientists of his day, he supervised the Virginia astronomers who extended the Mason-Dixon line into Ohio; designed a map of Virginia—"Madison's Map"—that remained standard for many years; conducted and published numerous investigations in astronomy, physics, geology, chemistry, and biology; and corresponded extensively with other American and British scientists. During his career in Williamsburg, he was solicited to be a candidate for the presidencies of King's College (now Columbia University), the University of Pennsylvania, Washington College (now Washington and Lee University), Transylvania University, and the College of Charleston.

Revered by his students, Bishop Madison taught not only natural science and mathematics, but also at various times moral philosophy, international law, and political economy. As president, he guided William and Mary with skill and devotion during the difficult period when it lost its endowment and government support following the Revolution. As bishop, he not only ordained more clergy in the first decade of his episcopate than any other Episcopal bishop of his time, but also tried

16

to reunite the Episcopal and Methodist Churches. Despite his efforts, he was obliged to watch the former Church of England in Virginia nearly die because of the social and political revolution that followed Independence. Viewed by many Virginians as the most eloquent preacher they had ever heard, Madison spoke with an impressive manner and in a learned, Ciceronian style. "A model of all the virtues social, domestic, and personal," the fourth President of the United States described him. On February 22, 1800, in the former capital of Virginia, Bishop James Madison was the natural choice to deliver the funeral eulogy for George Washington.

Seal of Bishop Madison.

Madison's memorial sermon proved an enormous success. Reprinted eight times by publishers as far north as Philadelphia and as far east as London, it represents a notable example of eighteenth-century American eloquence. The sermon continued to be published as long after Washington's death as 1844.

Taking his text from St. Paul and beginning with a reference to the nationwide mourning for the dead president, Madison proceeds to recount Washington's conspicuous achievements. He traces his career as military leader, statesman and chief magistrate, and private citizen. Throughout the oration he extolls Washington's many virtues, including "his temperance, his self-command in the heat of battle, his patience in sufferings, his prudence, his magnanimity, his ardent patriotism. . . ." (p.   ). The discourse ends with Madison urging his listeners to preserve the religious and moral qualities that Washington exemplified, so that at the "awful moment" of death they may, like him, exclaim "I have fought a good fight, I have finished my course, I have kept the faith." As the Bishop asserts in his dedication "To the Students of William and Mary College," George Washington is a model of moral worth, a figure they and other Americans should not only admire but also attempt to imitate.

As the twentieth-century reader approaches Bishop Madison's oration, he should visualize the scene at Bruton Parish Church in Williamsburg on February 22, 1800. He should imagine the organist, Peter Pelham, finishing a dead march. He should picture the communion table, the pulpit, and other parts of the church shrouded in black. He should see the hushed congregation of townspeople sitting in the high box pews and the professors and students of William and Mary sitting in the College galleries on the south and west walls. He should also imagine Bishop Madison—51 years old and silver-haired— ascending the tall pulpit. Because of the national period of mourning, Madison might have been dressed only in his black cassock with white tabs; but because of his belief in the Resurrection, he might also have been wearing his customary white surplice. Whatever his garb, he would have spoken earnestly, as was his custom, with few gestures.

The twentieth-century student of history should not so much read Bishop Madison's sermon on Washington as listen to it. Like John Tyler, he should listen for the rhythms and cadences of Madison's sentences, for the pauses with which he must have punctuated the sections of his oration, for the rise and fall of his voice. "Nothing could exceed the impressiveness of his reading," President Tyler wrote

> or the clearness and distinctness of his enunciation. The deep tones of his voice and its silvery cadence were incomparably fine. . . . I recollect nothing to equal the voice of Bishop Madison. No word was mouthed, no sentence im-

Pulpit, Bruton Parish Church, Williamsburg, VA.

perfectly uttered, but all was clear and distinct, and fell in harmony on the ear.

Ideally, the oration should be spoken aloud rather than read silently.

Americans interested in the life of George Washington will value Bishop Madison's funeral oration, for it represents perhaps the finest example of oratory delivered in the world at the time of Washington's death.

Sources and References

READERS will find an eyewitness account of George Washington's final days in *Letters and Recollections of George Washington: Being Letters of Tobias Lear and others ...* (New York, 1906), pp. 129-41. Lear, who was Washington's secretary, not only attended the former president throughout his final ordeal but also made the funeral arrangements. Washington's own brief record of his activities on December 12 and 13 is found in Donald Jackson and Dorothy Twohig, eds., *The Diaries of George Washington*, 6 vols. (Charlottesville, 1976-79), 6:378-79.

The standard modern biography of Washington is Douglas Southall Freeman *et al.*, *George Washington*, 7 vols. (New York, 1948-57.) The seventh volume in Freeman's series—John A. Carroll and Mary Wells Ashworth's *First in Peace* (New York, 1957—describes Washington's illness, death, and burial at length. Readers will find a briefer treatment of the last days in James T. Flexner's *George Washington*, 3 vols. (Boston, 1969), 3:456-62, in Richard Norton Smith's *Patriarch: George Washington and the New American Nation* (Boston, 1993), 351-354, and in Willard Sterne Randall's *George Washington: A Life* (New York, 1997). Lear's *Letters and Recollections* and Carroll and Ashworth's volume include thorough discussions of the diagnoses and treatment of Washington. For recent evaluations of the president's illness and the ability of the president's physicians, see Thomas M. Boyd "Death of a Hero, Death of a Friend: George Washington's Last Hours" *Virginia Cavalcade*, vol. 33, no. 4 (winter 1984), 136-143, and Peter Stavrakis "Heroic Medicine, Bloodletting, and the Sad Fate of George

Washington" *Maryland Medical Journal*, vol. 46, no. 10 (1997), 539-40.

The reaction of ordinary and prominent Americans to Washington's death is summarized in Carroll and Ashworth, pp. 648-53. Margaret B. Stillwell's *Washington Eulogies* (New York, 1916) illustrates the extent of popular mourning; John Marshall's *Life of George Washington*, 5 vols. (Philadelphia, 1804-07), 5:763-71, gives the most detailed account of official mourning. Henry Lee used the phrase "first in war, first in peace, and first in the hearts of his countrymen" in a funeral oration. The story of Washington and the cherry tree originated in Mason Locke Weems's *The Life of George Washington*, first published in 1800.

For Washington's special relationship with the College of William and Mary and Madison's career as professor and president there, see J. H. Morpurgo, *Their Majesties Royall Colledge* (Williamsburg, 1976) and Ludwell H. Johnson, III, "James Madison and the 'Long and Lingering Decline,' 1782-1812," in *The College of William and Mary: A History* (Williamsburg, 1993), 165-198. The most recent assessment of Madison as a bishop is found in David L. Holmes, *A Brief History of the Episcopal Church* (Valley Forge, 1993), 19-28. President Madison's two evaluations of his cousin may be found in James Madison, Jr., to Robert Walsh, 22 August 1831, in the James Madison, Jr., Papers in the Library of Congress. President Tyler's praise of Madison is found in his letter in William B. Sprague, ed., *Annals of the American Pulpit*, 9 vols. (New York, 1857-69), 5:321-22.

THE SYLE OF
BISHOP MADISON'S ORATION

ALTHOUGH to modern readers Bishop Madison's memorial oration may sound overly ornate and florid, its archaic quality stems not only from the change in literary style that occurred between the eighteenth and the twentieth centuries, but also from Madison's careful adherence to principles of rhetoric (the art of persuasive speech) rooted in ancient Greek and Latin oratory.

Unlike current American authors and speakers, eighteenth-century British and American writers and orators emphasized classical models and rules established by Greek and Roman orators. According to these rules, orations fell into three types—the *deliberative* (designed to persuade politically), the *forensic* (designed to persuade legally), and the *epideictic* (designed to praise, and occasionally—as in Marc Antony's speech over Caesar's body in Shakespeare's *Julius Caesar*—to blame). In his memorial sermon for Washington, Madison naturally chose to follow the rules appropriate to the epideictic type. Technically speaking, his oration was therefore an *encomium*.

Varying with the occasion and the subject, the rules of rhetoric followed by Bishop Madison also dictated whether an orator would speak in "high" (grand and inflated) style, in "middle" (formal but unpretentious) style, or in "low" (plain and colloquial) style. Since February 22, 1800, marked an occasion of solemn mourning for America's supreme hero, Madison naturally employed the high or "grand" style. Hence his sermon displays a "show" rhetoric, the kind orators since

Greek and Roman times had traditionally used in encomia to summarize the achievements and attributes of a leading figure of their time.

Today most American writers and speakers automatically use the middle or low style. "All modern literature," said Ernest Hemingway (who himself did much to simplify American literary style), "comes from one book by Mark Twain called *Huckleberry Finn.*"

Yet almost 200 years after George Washington's death, the high style remains familiar to Americans. We find it in the language of the King James Bible as well as in the tragedies of Shakespeare:

> What a piece of work is man! How noble in reason! How infinite in faculties! In form and moving how express and admirable! In action how like an angel! In apprehension how like a god! The beauty of the world, the paragon of the animals.

We find it in a speech that stampeded the 1896 Democratic national convention and caused the delegates to nominate William Jennings Bryan for president on the fifth ballot:

> You shall not press down upon the brow of labor this crown of thorns, you shall not crucify mankind upon a cross of gold.

We find it in William Faulkner's words upon accepting the Nobel Prize for literature in 1950:

> I believe that man will not merely endure: he will prevail. He is immortal, not only because he alone among creatures has an inexhaustible voice, but because he has a soul, a spirit capable of compassion and sacrifice and endurance.

Qualified by a purposeful use of small words, we find the high style as well in two of the most famous speeches delivered by American presidents—the first in 1863, the second in 1961:

> Four score and seven years ago our fathers brought forth on this continent a new nation, conceived in liberty, and dedicated to the proposition that all men are created equal. Now we are engaged in a great civil war, testing whether that nation, or any nation so conceived and so dedicated, can long endure...
>
> Let the word go forth from this time and place, to friend and foe alike, that the torch has been passed to a

24

new generation of Americans—born in this century, tempered by war, disciplined by a hard and bitter peace, proud of our ancient heritage...Now the trumpet summons us again—not as a call to bear arms, though arms we need—not as a call to battle, though embattled we are—but a call to bear the burden of a long twilight struggle, year in and year out...

By realizing the striking way in which Bishop Madison fulfills the rules to which the high style and the epideictic form bound him, twentieth-century readers can greatly enhance their appreciation of his sermon on Washington.

Throughout his oration, for example, Madison purposely employs language that is formal, learned, and occasionally archaic. Instead of using simple and familiar Anglo-Saxon words, he selects a stately diction of long, often Latinate words. Hence the reader will note that on page 31, Madison uses "spectacle" instead of "show" and "exalted" instead of "high;" on page 34, "plaudit" instead of "praise" and "augmented lustre" instead of "greater brightness;" and on page 39, "pecuniary compensation" instead of "pay" and "manifested" instead of "showed."

The Bishop's scholarly background and the high style account as well for the many words such as "monitions," "unconditional subjugation," "ignominious," "presentiment," "unbounded veneration," and "chimera" that occur throughout the sermon. For these reasons, too, he frequently alludes to such classical and Biblical figures as Hannibal, Scipio, Archimedes, Moses, Samson, Maccabeus, and Ananias.

In addition, throughout his oration Madison makes extensive use of tropes—figures of speech that, if taken literally, are simply untrue. Although Bishop Madison's tropes are not strikingly original, they were probably fresher in the eighteenth century than they are today. Taken together, they serve in the oration to embellish Washington's already high reputation, as in the following five examples:

Simile
The spirit of America like the daring eagle mounted as the storm advanced...(p. 40)

Metaphor

O! be thou, like him, thy country's shield in war, its ornament in peace. (p. 60)

Personification

Religion joins in the universal wo; she weeps over the
tomb of WASHINGTON. (p. 33)

Epithet

Perhaps his eagle-eye saw that this vast continent could
not long revolve round a small spot in the ocean. (p. 36)

Metonymy

At this awful moment, when the sword was to reek with
kindred blood, what were the agonizing pangs which
wrung every heart! (p. 40)

In keeping with his classical model, Madison not only begins
his oration with a rhetorical question (a question asked not to
elicit an answer but simply to emphasize a point), but also
scatters them throughout his text:

Who bears not in vivid memory the victors of Saratoga, or
him who rescued South Carolina from the fangs of the
lion? (p. 47)

When Washington becomes a preacher, who will not listen? (p. 57)

By frequently addressing his words to an absent person or to
a personified object or idea, Bishop Madison also employs
apostrophe. In the following examples he addresses and
hence evokes for his audience first the nation, then a county
in western Virginia, then a Revolutionary general, and finally
a British philosopher:

America, be thou Independent! Take thy place among
the nations of the earth! (p. 40)

Monongalia, thy proud forests first saw the youthful hero
impatient for the conflict...(p. 35)

Thou, too, lamented Mercer, shalt live immortal in the
memory of America. (p. 47)

Immortal Locke! Thine was the glory to arm the orator
with the sacred panoply of truth. (p. 38-39)

In addition, like many eighteenth-century authors, Bishop
Madison frequently uses hyperbole, or exaggeration for
effect:

The fatal battle in which Braddock fell was only the prelude to *those torrents of blood which flowed*...(p. 35)

...That mighty conflict which *shook the pillars of a distant throne.* (p. 34)
Then was heard the *thunder* of that eloquence which shook this continent. (p. 38)

Also typical of the high style is Madison's utilization of antithesis, or of long balanced constructions in which he matches clause with clause, phrase with phrase, or contrary with contrary, as in the following example:

To see WASHINGTON again at the head of the American people, no longer clad in armour, but seated in the curule chair, giving energy to the laws of the Union, and stability to the liberty he had vindicated, watching over the interests of all, harmonizing discordant states, establishing order and method in every department, and thus making a fair but grand experiment of the subserviency of the newly-created government to the general happiness, was a spectacle the most dignified, as well as the most grateful to every heart. (p. 54)

Most striking perhaps is Bishop Madison's recurrent use of the traditional rhetorical device of anaphora, where the same word or words begin a sequence of clauses or sentences:

I behold a young but enlightened people...I see the flame of an ardent love...I see a people but just beginning...I see, from this principle, this sincere love of virtue...It is thus they will defy the decrepitude of old age; it is thus they will be perpetually renovated in youth...it is thus they will show to the astonished world, that the love of virtue has snatched from death, amid his dread conquests, one victory more! (p. 31)

The model is classical, the style rich, the occasion solemn. Given the principles of rhetoric that governed at the time, no memorial oration delivered during the official period of mourning for America's first president surpassed in quality or in number of reprintings Bishop James Madison's *A Discourse on the Death of General Washington, Late President of the Unites States.*

NOTE: The 1800 text of Bishop Madison's oration has been reprinted with only one change. Because some of its paragraphs exceeded 900 words, the editor has divided them for modern readers.

BIBLIOGRAPHICAL ESSAY

WILBUR HOWELL's *Eighteenth-Century British Logic and Rhetoric* (Princeton, 1971) analyzes in detail the classical sources and subsequent development of rhetoric during the era of George Washington and Bishop Madison, as does Albert Furtwangler's *American Silhouettes: Rhetorical Identities of the Founders* (New Haven, 1987). The British rhetorical texts used most frequently in American colleges during the late eighteenth century were George Campbell's *Philosophy of Rhetoric*, 2 vols. (London, 1776) and Hugh Blair's *Lectures on Rhetoric and Belles Lettres*, 2 vols. (London, 1783). For a brief assessment of the influence of the classics on American political thought in the early national period, see Edwin A. Miles, "The Young American Nation and the Classical World," *Journal of the History of Ideas*, 35 (April-June 1974): 259-74 and John Zvesper "The American Founders and Classical Political Thought," *History of Political Thought*, vol. 10, no. 4 (1989), 701-718.

Readers will find the tribute to Twain in the first chapter of Hemingway's *Green Hills of Africa* (1935). The quotation from Shakespeare comes from Hamlet, II, ii, 317. The presidential speeches quoted are Abraham Lincoln's Gettysburg Address and John F. Kennedy's Inaugural Address.

A

DISCOURSE,

on the

DEATH

of

GENERAL WASHINGTON,

Late PRESIDENT *of the* UNITED

STATES;

DELIVERED

on the

22d of February, 1800,

In the Church in Williamsburg.

By JAMES MADISON, D. D.
*Bishop of the Protestant Episcopal Church in Virginia, and
President of* WILLIAM *and* MARY COLLEGE.

RICHMOND: PRINTED BY T. NICOLSON, JUST
BELOW THE CAPITOL.—1800.

COLLEGE OF WILLIAM AND MARY.
As it Stood from 1705 to 1859, When it was Burned.

To the Students of William and Mary College.

YOUNG GENTLEMEN,—To excel in moral worth, we must form an ideal model of moral perfection. To assist you in forming such a model has been my constant endeavour. With the same view I here present you with a real model; not as the standard of perfection; for that, like the beauty of bodies, is not to be discovered in any individual; but as an examplar of the happy combination of many of those moral beauties, which constitute the perfect character. Accept it as a small testimony of my affection; and be assured of my ardent prayers, that you may ever strive not only to equal, but to surpass it.

JAMES MADISON.

A DISCOURSE, &c.

I have fought a good fight, I have finished my course.—2 Tim. iv. 7.

Is there a spectacle under heaven so interesting to the human heart, as that of a free and numerous people putting on the ensigns of mourning, and, with one accord, pouring forth their sorrows for the loss they have sustained in the death of a beloved and honoured fellow citizen? Such is the spectacle which America this day presents. Glorious spectacle! Glorious to humanity, which has displayed virtues capable of exciting such universal, such heartfelt veneration and love! Glorious to you, citizens of America, who thus honour yourselves, by evincing the high value you entertain for exalted merit.

Great God! on this day, whose rising sun we of late hailed with joyful acclamations, as ushering in the morn which gave birth to the illustrious WASHINGTON, but which now, sad emblem of all things human, is set apart to bewail his loss, and to retrace the energies of his departed soul; on this day of wo, permit me to express the consolation which such a triumph of virtue excites within my heart.

I behold a young, but enlightened people, testifying, with one voice, their sincere devotion to virtue: I see the flame of an ardent love for what is truly great and good bursting forth from every bosom: I see a people but just beginning to move in their political orbit, giving the surest testimony that the love of virtue pervades the breast of every citizen, and that they possess a force which will retain them, throughout their long career, in the path of social felicity, and social greatness: I see, from this principle, this sincere love of virtue, the future glories of my country, already to commence.

It will be, if preserved in all its strength, the shield of liberty, the protecting angel of the republics of this western world: it will render them for ever illustrious for patriotism, for heroic deeds, for arts and for sciences. It is thus they will defy the decrepitude of old age; it is thus they will be perpetually renovated in youth; and, under the guidance of thy providence, O God, it is thus they will show to the astonished world, that the

WASHINGTON'S BIER.

love of virtue has snatched from death, amid his dread conquests, one victory more!

May this love be ever cherished with a holy zeal! May it ever be the distinguishing characteristic of Americans, to pay to it the homage which is due. May this day ever serve to recall the bright example of a WASHINGTON; and to renew, in the hearts of succeeding generations, that love for virtue which animates the present!

Ah! my friends and fellow-citizens, I am sensible of the difficulty of addressing you, upon this mournful occasion, in a manner correspondent to your feelings. But the love of my country, veneration for those rare qualities which dignify and ennoble man, and which diffuse such blessings throughout society; and, above all, the invitations of religion, give to me a momentary confidence. Those virtues which once animated the heroes of America in the day of battle, now animate the minister of religion, of truth, and of justice.

It is true, that genius and eloquence have already exerted their powers in calling to memory the splendid talents, the meritorious actions of the deceased, and that they have depicted them with a glow of colouring which I dare not attempt; but the subject can never become trite—it can never be exhausted. Let us, then, endeavour to retrace some of those qualities which distinguished our deceased fellow-citizen, as the hero, the patriot, and the sage; let us review some of the important scenes through which he passed; and let us search, for the grief we feel in his loss, a consolation in the recital of the wonders of his life.

It is a custom worthy of all free states, and which the most celebrated in antiquity religiously observed, "to be mindful of their ancestors, to extol them with merited panegyrics, and to honour them on such occasions as the present, that, by doing justice to the actions of the dead, they may excite the virtues of the living."

If, indeed, the illustrious WASHINGTON, whom all America deplores, and whom the whole civilized world will honour with their eulogies, had obtained only that celebrity, which extraordinary talents in war, in arts and sciences, or in politics, confer; if he had not been distinguished for his firm adherence to the truths of religion; if he had not served his God with a zeal worthy of his superior understanding, however full of glory he might have been in the eyes of man, Religion could not have added her voice to the general plaudit. But Religion joins in the universal wo: she weeps over the tomb of WASHINGTON! great in arms, great in peace, great in piety! and, amidst her sorrows, feels a gleam of consolation in pronouncing his eulogium.

I. With the life of WASHINGTON is connected a new æra in the history of man. He seems to have been called forth by Heaven, as the instrument of establishing principles fundamental in social happiness, and which must and will pervade the civilized world.

When young, he was trained to hardihood and to arms; he was educated in the school of war, and thus prepared for that mighty conflict which shook the pillars of a distant throne. The government which nursed the youthful warrior, nursed a Sampson, who was one day to break its fetters, and burst its cords asunder. Virginia saw in her youthful son traits of that character which was to become the admiration of the world; the morning of his life gave the well founded hope, that the meridian of his day would shine with augmented lustre, and that his setting sun would leave a long tract of glory behind. Great talents soon manifest themselves by the force with which

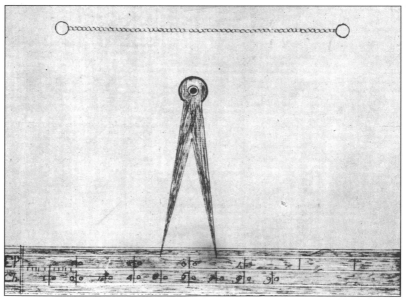

The chain, compass and scale were drawn by George Washington when he was
14 years old.

they take their direction. "David, when a youth, sought out the lion and the bear as subjects for his valour, and voluntarily joined himself to the armies of Israel, to be instructed in the arts of war." WASHINGTON sought out the warrior of the wilderness, and, at an early age, provoked his courage and his stratagems.*

Monongalia, thy proud forests first saw the youthful hero impatient for the conflict; saw him firm and undaunted amid superior foes; saw him snatch from an entire destruction the shattered remnant of a brave but ill-conducted army.

The fatal battle in which Braddock fell was only the prelude to those torrents of blood which flowed from the contest of two vast but rival powers. WASHINGTON, now commander of all the forces raised in Virginia, continued the career of military glory which he had so happily commenced, until his constitution, naturally strong and robust, became debilitated by incessant fatigue and the unusual hardship to which he was exposed. He was thus compelled to retire from the service of his country, attended with the sincere regret of all his companions in arms. But this retirement was only a preparation for the august theatre upon which he was afterwards to appear. It would be delightful could we attend him in this retirement; could we here trace out the steps which his philosophic mind pursued in the acquisition of useful knowledge.

Hitherto, Turenne, Marlborough, and Eugene, had been his

---

*General WASHINGTON was born on the 22d of February, 1732, N. S. When a youth, he was entered a midshipman on board a British vessel of war, but relinquished his nautical views, in consequence of the entreaties of his friends. Before he attained his twentieth year, he was appointed Adjutant of one of the three districts into which Virginia was then divided, with the rank of Major. In his 21st year he was sent, by Governor Dinwiddie, with plenary powers to examine into the encroachments reported to have been made by the French and Indians, on the frontiers of Virginia; to treat with the latter, and to warn the former against future aggressions. His journal and report to the Governor have been published. The next year, 1754, he was appointed Colonel of a Regiment, raised for the defence of the frontiers; signalized himself at Fort-Necessity by a sally, in which he defeated an army much superior to his own. In 1755 he acted as Aid-de-camp to General Braddock, and attended him, in that capacity, in the battle in which he fell. Not an officer whose duty obliged him to be mounted that day, except Colonel WASHINGTON escaped death or wounds. The conducting of the retreat devolved upon him; it was effected with a judgment which acquired him a high reputation, both in Great-Britain and America. Such was the fatigue he underwent on the day of action, and the succeeding night, that he was obliged, the next morning, to be supported on his preceptors. I know with what ardency, in the early stage of his life, he followed them through every campaign, retraced their battles, and thus served under those illustrious men. WASHINGTON has often been supposed to have made a Camillus, a Fabius, or an Emilius, his prototype. I believe that he was himself destined to be a high example to mankind, and that the native strength of his own mind soared above imitation; but still it is probable, that his knowledge in tactics was greatly perfected during this period of retirement, by cultivating an acquaintance with the most distinguished commanders of ancient and modern times.

Nor can it be doubted that politics, the true principles of all lawful governments, and especially the rights and interests of America, often occupied his active and penetrating mind. No one had a firmer hold of the chain of causes and effects. No one saw with more clearness the astonishing progress of America in population and in wealth, or better knew how to estimate the operating causes. Perhaps his eagle-eye saw that this vast continent could not long revolve round a small spot in the ocean. But, whatever may have been the presentiment of his mind, it is certain that in this retirement he cultivated all those social virtues which attach man to man, and faithfully discharged those duties which a good citizen owes to his country; nor is it less certain, that he continued, without interruption, the active friend of religion, and at no time forgetful of his God.

During this retirement, a blind policy was preparing the way for an event the most important in the annals of the world. It is wonderful to consider how often the agency of causes, which men put in motion, produce results the most opposite to their intentions, and which baffle all calculation. Ambition forms her plans of subjugation, and anticipates her triumphs; but they are controlled by an all-wise and over-ruling Providence. Instead of

---

horse with cushions. The government of Virginia, soon after this period, gave him the command of all the troops raised, and to be raised, in the colony. He defended the frontiers with skill and judgment, until the year 1758. In this year he commanded the Van-Brigade of General Forbes, in the capture of Fort DuQuesne. By this campaign tranquillity was restored to the frontiers of Virginia. The health of Colonel WASHINGTON being greatly impaired, he resigned his military appointments in 1759.

George Washington, Charles Willson Peale, 1772.

oppression and misery, there often spring forth liberty, social order, and social happiness.

That war, in which WASHINGTON had taken his first lessons in the military art, was concluded in the year 1761. "The prosperity of the American colonies had continued to flow with a quick current amid all the devastations of war." The progress of population, of commerce, of improvement in the most useful of all arts, agriculture, had received an impulse which could not be restrained. "An enthusiastic affection for the parent country had taken deep root." The sons of America had fought and conquered with the armies of Britain. "Their feelings and their interests had been interwoven with new strength" during the hour of danger and the triumphs of victory. But the tide of affection did not long continue at the height to which it had risen. An attempt, in 1764, to tax America in a manner unconstitutional, and incompatible with political liberty, aroused the vigilance of the colonies.

At this crisis, observe, fellow-citizens, Virginia first saw the lurking poison, and first dared to propose the first American Congress that ever met. At her request it met at New York in 1765. By the wisdom and the firmness of that Congress, the particular measure which had excited such irritation in America was abandoned.

But the abandonment was attended with a declaration, that the right of Britain to bind America by laws and statutes was unlimited, or extended to all cases whatever. An assumption of power, so big with disgrace and ruin, was viewed by America with horror and indignation. In vain did reason and eloquence, on both sides of the Atlantic, demonstrate and deplore the calamities which would ensue from an attempt to enforce this assumed right. It was attempted. The patriotism of Boston foiled the attempt, and whelmed the insidious bait into the briny deep.

Infatuated councils saw not that an obstinate perseverance in this mad system of political ambition, would give to the world an example the most instructive; an example which would rouse nations from their lethargy, show to them their own strength, teach them those primeval rights which men hold only from nature's charter, and awake the spirit to vindicate them. Then was the voice of Henry heard! then was heard the thunder of that eloquence which shook this continent! His great soul, burning with the concentered rays of wisdom and of patriotism, first proclaimed the meditated treason against the majesty of the people.

Immortal Locke! thine was the glory to arm the orator with

Stamp Act Protests.

the sacred panoply of truth. Nor to him alone were thy energies confined. Thy hallowed page, dear to liberty, to virtue, and to religion, shed intellectual light over this western world, and taught a lesson congenial to the first sentiments of man. The American mind, too, nursed in the bosom of Independence, spurned any other controul than that which was founded on legitimate government. At this eventful crisis, Virginia again stood foremost in the cause of liberty.

Like another Athens watching over the safety of all Greece, and inspiring courage by her councils, Virginia first proposed a Congress of the different States. It met; a dreadful appeal to heaven drew near; a day of mourning and intercession was appointed, and observed with an awful solemnity. "God! give the people one heart and one mind, firmly to oppose every invasion of American rights," was the prayer then enjoined and addressed to the throne of grace. In vain were the reasonings and the entreaties of that august assembly of statesmen, patriots and heroes, who were now consulting for the general interests of America, and who so eminently distinguished themselves for their moderation, their firmness, and their wisdom. Whose breast is so callous as not to be touched with the noble sentiments, the profound reasoning, the manly, energetic style, the sacred ardour, in the cause of liberty, which have immortalized their records! They are examples to all generations, and will remain, for ever, monuments of human genius and human virtue.

Virginia saw that the moment had arrived when the rights of freemen, Heaven's sacred gift, were to be yielded, or defended with a courage worthy of such a prize. "To die," she said "is common to all, but to die bravely is peculiar to few. Let us not, then, regard our lives as what properly belongs to us; but by exposing them to the public cause, let us acquire a renown which shall be peculiar and truly our own. Let us again prove, that an handful of freemen, contending for their rights, is more powerful than a host, numerous as the sands of the sea, labouring with infamy to infringe them."

A third time she rose in all the strength of liberty, and first proposed the Declaration of Independence. Nay, she alone, with a patriotic courage, which astonishes even at this day, took the bold resolution to sever herself from Britain, and to meet every danger in defence of her rights. The great council of America soon saw the necessity of a similar decision. America, be thou Independent! take thy place among the nations of the earth! was the high decree. Nor let it be forgot, that the voice of WASHINGTON sanctioned the decree. To arms! to arms! re-echoed throughout the Continent.

At this awful moment, when the sword was to reek with kindred blood, what were the agonizing pangs which wrung every heart! Ah! ye whom the hand of Providence hath still preserved to this day, ye can tell; ye can recall the memory of times which tried men's souls. But the spirit of America, like the daring eagle, mounted as the storm advanced, pierced the thick clouds with inbred lightning fraught, and, from aloft beheld the promised land of liberty and peace.

It was then America hailed WASHINGTON as her conductor through the tempests of war. Like the chosen leader of the Israelites, reposing in his God, he obeyed the voice. To him it was ever sacred.

But what were his feelings at this moment! The sea of

troubles, through which he must pass, lay before him. On one side he saw vast superiority in numbers, wealth unbounded, lust of domination insatiable, armies inured to war and conquest, fleets which waved their triumphant banners over the ocean, and which vexed, with their prows, the most distant seas: on the other, he saw a people thinly scattered over an extensive continent, without arms, without funds, without a regular government to concentre their force, without fleets; with no other allies than their own courage, their virtuous oaths, their love of liberty, and their confidence in the righteousness of their cause!

But, ardent in the defence of the rights of his country, animated with the true spirit of exalted patriotism, he implored the assistance of heaven, and hastened to the post assigned him. Never was there one more perilous. Never was there one which so called for all those great qualities of the soul, which command the admiration of the world. Never was there a trust reposed on which depended issues so momentous. On the wisdom, the integrity, the prudence, the fortitude of one man, hung the destiny of this western world.

True glory is always modest and simple. Nothing but the noble principle of obedience to the will of his country could have induced him to accept such a trust, or to appear as the chief vindicator of American liberty. His magnanimity was no less evinced by not declining the immense weight of the office to which he had been called, than his disinterestedness was by a refusal to accept any pecuniary compensation during the war.

No sooner had he arrived at the American army, than he diffused order through every department. The same greatness of soul which attended him throughout the war, manifested itself in the wisdom of his first arrangements, and the measures which he took to expel the enemy from Boston. Success crowned his efforts.

But trials, which might have shaken the soul of a Joshua, a Maccabeus, or an Epaminondas, now awaited him. An hostile army, the most formidable in numbers, in discipline, in all the apparatus of war, commanded by a general brave, skilful and enterprising, had landed on our shores. It was now that the horrors of war were to rage in all their fury, and the plains of America to be drenched with human blood. Ah! soon did those horrors commence.

Misfortune, for a long time, hovered round the banners of America. In vain did patriotism animate troops half disciplined, half armed, and inferior in number. From Long Island, from New-York, and through the Jerseys, discomfiture attended the American arms. Yet, amid these defeats, a courage was displayed, which was worthy of the first efforts of men struggling in the cause of humanity. Full many a hoary father wept the untimely fate of his gallant son. Full many a widowed matron was left the sad monument of wo. Fathers, mothers, wives, ye too, tender babes, whose tongues had just learned to lisp a father's name, your virtuous tears flowed not in vain; they plead with angel eloquence in their country's cause. Heaven itself saw and pitied the sufferings, and the impending dangers of America.

Driven from Long Island, beyond the Delaware, his army reduced to a few brave and faithful compatriots, despondence and dismay marked every countenance, except that of WASHINGTON. Superior to events, which seemed more than sufficient to shake the stoutest hearts, they served only to arouse, and to call forth the strength of WASHINGTON's genius.

It was in this season of weakness, of despondency and dismay, when the rigour of winter seemed to oppose insurmountable obstacles, when the spirit of Delaware's angry flood shrieked loud, and threatened destruction, that WASHINGTON, attended by a few faithful heroes, formed the bold resolution to defy every difficulty, to cross the enraged flood, to attack the victorious foe, and to snatch from him an immortal victory, in the midst of his triumphs. The design was formed and executed with a celerity, a judgment, and a fortitude, which was crowned with complete success. This was the first moment that presented the possibility of victory. It was seized.

The bold and gallant achievement astonished the enemy, revived the American spirit, and opened the door to still greater enterprise. Reinforcements succeeded this first victory. WASHINGTON returned to Trenton, where he had just acquired so much glory. The active enemy, breathing revenge for their late misfortune, hasten also to the same place, and arrive on the same evening, with a force greatly superior. The setting sun beheld Trenton containing the two hostile armies, separated only by a small stream.

What a crisis! The returning light of the next morn threatened a period to the hopes of America. Destruction or captivity seemed inevitable. Scarce could the brave sons of America refrain from censuring the rashness of their commander. They cast their eyes upon each other, upon their arms, and upon

Washington Crossing the Delaware, 1776.

43

their country. "The scoffs of the conquerors; their haughty looks, when, disarmed, they should be led through the hostile lines;" the loathsome jail, or the murderous prison-ship, all arose before their eyes. One consolation remained. They could die in defence of their country.

But the genius of WASHINGTON, ever invigorated by difficulties, here displayed its native force. A situation so perilous, was to him only the means of acquiring new glory. "A retreat would have been ignominious, a battle fatal."

See the event. At the return of day, a moment which his enemy had so anxiously anticipated, WASHINGTON was a conqueror on the plains of Princeton. He who appeared destined to certain captivity, was thundering upon his enemy in a distant quarter, and gaining new laurels.

I do not say this this exploit was worthy of the sagacity of an Hannibal, or the wisdom of a Scipio. It was worthy of WASHINGTON; it will be itself an example to succeeding ages, and will forever retain the full verdure of glory. A kind Providence forwarded, in an astonishing manner, an enterprise the most distinguished for that quickness of penetration which enables great minds to convert circumstances, apparently the most inauspicious, into such as are most favourable. This brilliant victory evinced the deep resources of WASHINGTON's mind, and excited the universal admiration and applause of a people who loved and revered him; whilst his enemy saw, and had the generosity to acknowledge, the pre-eminence of talents, so dangerous to themselves, but so invaluable to his country.

Can we look back with cold indifference upon events so recent, at which the American heart once rebounded with joy, felt the full debt of gratitude to Heaven, and fervently expressed that gratitude in praise and thanksgiving? Can we forget the man whom Heaven selected as the instrument of its loving-kindness towards us? No; sooner shall gratitude cease to be a virtue! sooner shall the love and admiration of heroic deeds, of all those exalted talents which give dignity to man, be obliterated from the human breast!

Thus did a campaign, which, in its beginning, threatened unconditional subjugation, in its end, present a prospect the most animating and consolatory to the friends of liberty. The cause of America had now attracted the attention of the world. Her armies had evinced a spirit worthy of such a cause: her enemies had been compelled to retrace their path of victory, whilst WASHINGTON, tranquil in danger, sure in council, superior in his views and resources, had acquired the unbounded love, veneration and confidence of his fellow soldiers, had commanded the respect of his enemies, and proved that he was worthy of the high trust committed to him.

It was this love, this veneration, this confidence, daily increasing, as his talents and his virtues were more and more developed, which formed the treasury of America. Yes, ye brave and virtuous defenders of your country, ye companions of the illustrious WASHINGTON, I call you to witness, that, amid all your sufferings, this devotion to your chief was your bond of union, your support, and your reward! Whether ye lay untented on the frozen earth, or marked your way by the blood-stained ground on which ye trod, or caught, in haste, a scanty morsel; still, amidst all your privations, your attachment to your commander, founded on the just admiration of his heroic virtues, supported you in every trial, consoled you under every difficulty, and animated you with a patriotic enthusiasm in the day of battle.

This command of the affections of brave and virtuous men; this entire possession of the heart of every soldier; this unbounded veneration for their chief, whilst it forms the greatest glory of a general, converts each soldier into a hero! He seizes, as an example for himself, the great model which his general exhibits. His temperance, his self-command in the heat of battle, his patience in sufferings, his prudence, his magnanimity, his ardent patriotism, infuse themselves into every breast, give an elevation to the mind, a dignity, a confidence, a spirit, which converts man into a new being, communicates to every power a new energy, and creates a force wonderful and irresistible.

Such was the agency of WASHINGTON's genius. It possessed a creative power, which assimilated every thing to itself; or, which called forth in others talents they felt not before. His very presence inspired fortitude. No one approached him, but felt the spirit of heroism transfused into his bosom. I think I see, at this moment, the brave soldier, as he passes, hail him as his father, friend and champion; I think I see him rise to redeem his country, exult in his martial exercise, and with a holy fervency calling down blessings on his commander's honoured head; pant again to fight for freedom, or for freedom die!

But if WASHINGTON had hitherto discovered talents wonderfully great in seizing, with promptitude, the first avenues to success, or of profiting from the smallest inadvertence of a general, deservedly high in military estimation, the time had now arrived when the caution of a Fabius, or rather a caution so peculiar to himself, was to be displayed. His inferiority in numbers, and in all the equipments of war, compelled him to take a position on the strong grounds of Morristown. It is doubtful whether he manifested greater talents as a commander, in this situation, or in those scenes of brilliant action which we have just mentioned.

No one knew better the value of that golden curb which discretion hangs on bravery. A general engagement, which the enemy so ardently solicited, would, in all probability, have extinguished, forever, the bright flame of liberty. To the invading army, procrastination was defeat. In vain did the impetuosity of the American councils urge him to battle. Nothing could move the soul of WASHINGTON but the spirit of wisdom, which, ever calm and serene, had determined him now to be content with checking the movements of the enemy, and to maintain a war of caution. It was this caution, so full of prudence and military skill, which, continually baffling the designs of the enemy, compelled them to embark, and to attempt to gain Philadelphia by sea.

The attempt forced WASHINGTON from his strong posts. The battle of Brandywine ensued. The valour of our troops was unshaken, but the event was not fortunate for the American arms. "There are casualties which human prudence cannot always control, but upon which the issues of battles often depend." One of these occurred. A false intelligence prevented the execution of a design, the most bold in its nature; but so admirably planned, that, had an attempt been made to carry it into effect, victory, and not defeat, would have been the result.

Nor were the actions of Germantown and of Monmouth less signalized for the skill of the general, and the valour of his troops, than for those untoward events which defeated their hopes. WASHINGTON had not always the glory of success, but he had the glory of appearing to deserve it. The wisdom of his measures was never doubted; success, O God! depends upon thy providence.

But, fellow citizens, we should not do justice to the talents, or the virtues of WASHINGTON, were we to confine our view to those scenes only in which he himself was the principal actor. During the progress of a war, which raged from the frozen walls of Quebec to the burning sands of Savannah, the penetrating eye of WASHINGTON saw every movement; his comprehensive mind took in the vast whole; his councils were received as the monitions of an oracle; whilst, from his example, sprung up heroes in every quarter. The enemy had soon, every where, if not a WASHINGTON to contend with, at least one who gloried in following the exalted model. His knowledge of human nature gave him the command of talents wherever they appeared; whilst his magnanimity rendered him always the first to announce the merit of others, and to participate in their triumphs.

Whose bosom glows with the virtuous pride of being a citizen of America, and remembers not the gallantry of Greene at Redbank; or the noble defence of Smith at Mud-Island? Who bears not in vivid memory the victors of Saratoga, or him who rescued South Carolina from the fangs of the lion? Who calls not to mind the brave, the virtuous, but unfortunate Fayette?

Thou, too, lamented Mercer, shalt live immortal in the memory of America. Thy wounds, received in the bloody contest which preceded the revolutionary war, had already evinced thy courage and thy patriotism. Ah! weltering in thy blood, abandoned in the midst of the inhospitable wilderness, the deadly serpent thy only food, what but a kind Providence could have preserved thee from such perils! It did preserve thee, long to live the delight of society, and to become the firm vindicator of liberty. Yes, the hand of God preserved thee, again to unite thy arms with WASHINGTON, and to pour forth thy gallant, but gentle soul, on the plains of Princeton, covered with glory.

Would time permit, I could here, with that joy which the love of noble deeds inspires, trace a long line of heroes, whose names will be for ever dear to America, and whose energies WASHINGTON saw, combined, and thus produced a force, constant in its action, and irresistible in its effects. Recall the image of this illustrious man; behold him, when not braving the dangers of the field, seated in council, deep deliberation engraven on his countenance; see him giving life and motion to distant armies, and incessantly directing every thing to the political salvation of his country. He seems another Archimedes, sitting on the shore, and moving, at pleasure, a vast ship, on an ocean tossed with tempest, whilst he himself is immovable.

A just eulogium of WASHINGTON requires a detail of the actions of his life. The wonderful properties, the inimitable beauties of those rays which enlighten and animate all nature, to be seen in their full lustre, must be viewed separately. But this detail, this separated view of the luminous actions of WASHINGTON, must be left to the judicious and impartial historian. The time with which you have already favoured me, admonishes me to hasten to that scene of glory which still awaited our beloved fellow-citizen, and which, by closing the bloody drama, established, we trust in God, for ever, pure republicanism in this western world.

That last scene was reserved for Virginia. Her favourite son was destined, in her bosom, to receive the reward of all his toils, and to finish, in her sight, his career of military glory. I will not open wounds which are but just healed; I will not awake the feelings of the friend, the orphan, or the parent; nor will I call to mind the accumulated distress which mourned throughout this land. Suffice it to say, that a superior and a gallant foe, the conqueror of India, spread terror and desolation on every side.

WASHINGTON saw the decisive moment; he saw that providence had, at length, presented the opportunity of closing the sufferings of his country. With a decision, a profoundness of judgment, which astonishes, he projected, and formed, with his brave and generous allies, a plan apparently the most difficult in its execution, and which, to common apprehension, would have indicated only the feebleness of vanity and folly. A powerful enemy in New-York was to be kept in a state of alarm for his safety; allied troops were to be assembled at the same moment, not only from a distant quarter on the Continent, but from Islands still more remote; a fleet, which gallantly aided in the great design, was to second every movement, and to assume its place at the appointed time; his own troops, by rapid marches, were to ensure their arrival at the period affixed; the militia of Virginia, provisions of all kinds, were to be collected.

How many powers were here to be combined! What difficulty in their arrangement! What prudence in adjusting means so discordant! What secrecy in the execution!

The mind of WASHINGTON was superior to every difficulty. The hostile army beheld themselves surrounded by a force, which ensured their captivity, before they suspected the design. Nothing more clearly evinces the strength of mind which this extraordinary man possessed, than the sure calculation which he had made of the result of all his measures, and also of the consequences which would attend the success of this bold but well concerted enterprise.

Weak minds, ever vacillating, find their emblem in the aspin's leaf. They have no centre of repose. That of WASHINGTON was self-poised; it felt its own weight, rested upon its own determinations.

The admiral of the allied forces hesitated whether he should keep the station assigned to him. America should often review the letter which WASHINGTON wrote to him from this city. Hear it, fellow-citizens:—"I am unable to describe the painful anxiety under which I have laboured since the reception of your letter. It obliges me *warmly* to urge a perseverance in the plan agreed upon. The attempt upon York, under the protection of your shipping, is as certain of success as a superior force, and a superiority of measures, can render any military operation. The capture of the British army is a matter so important in itself, and *in its consequences,* that is must greatly tend to put an end to the war." After pointing out the certain and fatal event which would follow the removal of the allied fleet, he adds, "I earnestly beg your Excellency to consider, that, if by moving your fleet from the situation agreed upon, we lose the present opportunity, we shall never hereafter have it in our power to strike so decisive a blow, and the period of an honourable peace will be farther distant than ever." He then assures the admiral, that he had nothing to fear from the fleet of the enemy, however superior, stationed as he was; and then concludes, "I am to press your Excellency to persevere in the scheme so happily concerted between us." This letter was the anchor of victory. WASHINGTON, with his brave allies, advanced to York. They came, they saw, they conquered!

Then did America exclaim, "If God be for us, who can be against us!" Yes, great God! then was thy providential kindess manifested; then was it felt and adored by all; but by none with more ardour, or more humility, than by him who had been selected as the chief instrument in thy hands, for the establishment of liberty in this new world. "Let," said he, "divine service be performed to-morrow in the different brigades and divisions. The commander in chief recommends, that all the troops which are not upon duty, do assist at it with a serious deportment, and *that sensibility of heart, which the recollection of the surprising and particular interposition of Providence in our favour claims.*" His thanks are then tendered to the whole army in the warmest language; and let it be rememberd, that the militia of Virginia, with their governor and general, the virtuous and the patriotic Nelson, received, in a particular manner, his sincere acknowledgements of their brave and zealous co-operation.

Joy, like the rapid lightning, ran from one extremity of the Continent to the other. Every house of public worship resounded with grateful praises and thanksgivings to the God of battles. Every heart called forth blessings on the head of WASHINGTON. Every American now began to hail the glorious consummation of all his hopes. The vindicators of liberty now saw that the storm which had so long desolated their country, and deluged it with blood, was rapidly subsiding: the horizon began to gleam around, and promised the speedy effulgence of the brightest day which ever illuminated this earth.

Washington Arriving in New York, 1789.

That day soon arrived. It was the day which witnessed the acknowledgement of the freedom, the sovereignty, and the independence of the different states of America.

Is the orb of WASHINGTON's glory now full? No! it is increasing in splendour. How many victors have found a Rubicon, whose small current only tempted its passage: and, when once passed, how oft has a mad ambition tossed the laws and liberties of the people in the air!

The integrity of WASHINGTON was a rock, in the midst of the ocean, which could not be moved. His patriotism was as firm as the continent he had saved. He was now to give another example to succeeding ages, another proof of the reality and the greatness of his virtues.

By his prudence he first drew off silently the wrath of military tumult: it was an angry cloud, which might have been terrific to his country, had not WASHINGTON, like the immortal Franklin, known how to avert its fury. No sooner had the veterans of America, unrecompensed as they were for all their labours and their sufferings, resumed the character of citizens, than their beloved commander repaired to Congress.

Behold him, fellow-citizens, in this exalted act of patriotic duty. See him with a modesty and dignity of manners so peculiar to himself, rising in the august council of America, delivering an address replete with the noblest sentiments, and unrobing himself of all his military authority. "Happy," said he, "in the confirmation of our independence and sovereignty, and pleased with the opportunity afforded the United States of becoming a respectable nation, I resign, with satisfaction, the appointment I accepted with diffidence; a diffidence in my abilities to accomplish so arduous a task; which, however, was superseded by a confidence in the rectitude of our cause, the support of the supreme power in the union, and the patronage of heaven.

"The successful termination of the war has verified the most sanguine expectations; and my gratitude for the interposition of Providence, and the assistance I have received from my countrymen, increases with every review of the momentous contest." He concludes with saying, "I consider it as an indispensable duty to close this last act of my official life, by commending the interests of our dear country to the protection of Almighty God, and those who have the superintendence of them to his holy keeping. Having now finished the work assigned, I retire from the great theatre of action, and, bidding an affectionate farewell to this august body, under whose orders I have so long acted, I here offer my commission, and take my leave of all the employments of public life."

The thousand emotions, which crowded upon the minds of all present, rendered the scene awfully impressive. The answer of the President was delivered with a sensibility which almost suppressed utterance. It was a just tribute to the many virtues, military and civil, of the illustrious WASHINGTON, and deserves to be engraved upon his tomb.

The acclamations of a grateful country, the applause and the admiration of the world, attended him to the peaceful walks of private life. Tyranny only trembled at the lesson he had taught; a lesson, said the President of Congress, equally useful to those who inflict, and to those who feel oppression. Yes, fellow-citizens, the eloquent lesson which he taught, caused those scales with which the false lustre of power had obscured the vision of men to drop from their eyes. The American revolution, like another Ananias, seems to have been sent by Heaven to open the eyes of the universe.

Hitherto, fellow-citizens, you have admired the departed, but immortal WASHINGTON, as a commander. Follow his steps still further, and you will equally admire him as the statesman and the sage.

WASHINGTON'S BOOK-PLATE

Mount Vernon.

II. When the interests of America indicated a closer union of those sovereignties which the revolution had established, Virginia, ever watchful over the general prosperity, and faithful to her principles, again stood foremost. This is the fourth time that she first suggested to her equals the adoption of measures which were essential to the liberties, the prosperity, and the aggrandizement of all. Great God! we thank thee that reason, and not arms, is the force which hath hitherto directed the political movements of a virtuous and enlightened people. The general council, which was proposed, met; WASHINGTON was again called into the service of his country, and unanimously elected president of an assembly of men illustrious for their talents and their patriotism.

From this assembly emanated the present constitution of the Federal Government. He, who never solicited an office, was solicited by all America to accept the important office of President of the United States. With what diffidence he received this testimony of the confidence, the love, and the veneration of a free and independent people, is in the memory of every one; nor is the exultation, which spread like the break of morning light, less strongly recollected.

To see WASHINGTON again at the head of the American people, no longer clad in armour, but seated in the curule chair, giving energy to the laws of the Union, and stability to the liberty he had vindicated, watching over the interests of all, harmonizing discordant states, establishing order and method in every department, and thus making a fair but grand experiment of the subserviency of the newly-created government to the general happiness, was a spectacle the most dignified, as well as the most grateful to every heart.

With what assiduity he devoted himself to the duties of his office; with what consummate prudence and judgment he directed the legitimate powers entrusted to him to their proper ends, let the voice of his country declare! Let the policy pursued, whilst Europe, maddening with contention, was convulsed to her centre, and whilst conflicting nations were labouring to plunge this country into the whirlpool of war, testify the wisdom, the magnanimity, and the patriotism of its conductor. Peace with all nations, close connexions with none, union among ourselves, measures favourable to commercial intercourse, both internal and external, a militia properly organized, not extensive military establishments, institutions to develope and to extend the powers of the intellect, and to diffuse knowledge; these were the objects which engaged his attention, and formed the basis of his policy.

During his administration, it is true, that parties, the concomitants of all free governments, arose. WASHINGTON, too, had his party; it was that of the public good. He was the chief magistrate of a whole nation, and not of a part of that nation. Onward he bent his steady course, inflexible in the pursuit of what he deemed just and proper; conscious of his own integrity; relying upon the favour of heaven; and affording an example of that rare assemblage, or rather constellation of virtues, which will and must be the admiration of ages.

Was, then, WASHINGTON exempt from error? This I do not say. He was a man; and, consequently, had the infirmities of man. But this I do believe, and think the whole tenor of his life justifies the belief—that, if he did err, his errors were never intentional. Human wisdom and human virtue claim no higher prerogative. To Heaven only infallibility belongs.

But though WASHINGTON may have erred, he had the merit of extracting glory even from his errors. How worthy of a great soul are the following sentiments, which he delivers in his last address: "Though," says he, "in reviewing the incidents of my administration, I am unconscious of intentional error, I am, nevertheless, too sensible of my defects not to think it probable that I may have committed many errors. Whatever they may be, I fervently beseech the Almighty to avert or mitigate the evils to

THE VIRGINIA GAZETTE.

—RICHMOND—
FRIDAY, DECEMBER 20, 1799.

DIED,

After a short and severe illness, on Saturday last, at his seat of Mount Vernon,

GEORGE WASHINGTON,

in the 68th year of his age.
——————Still be the Voice of Mirth! Hush'd be all Sounds of Joy! In silent Sorrow mourn Columbia, mourn! If Loss of Worth unequalled here below, be Cause of Grief a Cause of Woe and Grief unbounded, bids thee mourn——thy worthiest, noblest Son is no more—ILLUSTRIOUS WASHINGTON is dead! —Awful Truth! Heart piercing Soun! It shocks where e'er 'tis heard! It stops the invidious Tongue, and makes e'en party sleep.——Ye noble Shades of antient Greece and Rome, who dwell where endless Bliss is found, receive Columbia's Pride.—Conduct him to the highest Seat amongst you, so long designed for him—and you Illustrious Shades of human Excellence, go add thy Virtues to that noble Band.——To attempt to speak his smallest Praise, would be to attempt to paint the Splendour of the Sun.

At a very early period of his life, in the war of 1755, he gave signal proofs of that superior military genius, which afterwards was so usefully and gloriously displayed in the conduct of the war, which ended in freeing the United States from the dominion of Great Britain.

The object being accomplished for which America had taken up arms, on the establishment of peace and the acknowledgment of its independence, he resigned his commission, and returned to private life—covered with the grateful applauses of his country, and the admiration of mankind—but not without first giving them a further proof of his zeal to secure and perpetuate that liberty, which his prowess, aided by the spirit of his countrymen, had so happi-

56

which they may tend. I shall also carry with me the hope, that my country will never cease to view them with indulgence; and that forty-five years of my life having been dedicated to its service, with an upright zeal, the faults of incompetent abilities will be consigned to oblivion, as myself must soon be to the mansions of rest."

Twice called to the presidential office, his fellow-citizens waited only for the return of that day, on which they should exercise the sovereign right of election, again to clothe him with the same honours. But, more anxious to enjoy the rights of a private citizen than the honours of office; wearied, too, with the long and laborious service, which had constantly occupied his mind; and desirous to spend the evening of his day in domestic tranquillity, he announced his intention of retiring.

He did not, however, forget that he still owed to his country an important duty. This was discharged by an address worthy of WASHINGTON. It contains the outlines of the policy he pursued when in office, and which I have attempted slightly to sketch. It contains, also, admonitions the most wise, founded on long experience and deep reflection; admonitions which ought to be indelibly imprinted upon the mind of every American. It is the advice of the father of American liberty, no less illustrious as a statesman and a sage, than as a commander in war. America, hear this sentence: "Of all the dispositions and habits which tend to political prosperity, religion and morality are indispensable supports. In vain would that man claim the tribute of patriotism, who should labour to subvert those great pillars of human happiness, those firmest props of the duties of men and citizens. The mere politician ought to respect and cherish them. A volume could not trace their connexion with private and public felicity."

The mind of WASHINGTON saw, that republicanism without morality was a chimera; and that morality without religion was as evanescent as the baseless fabric of a vision: he saw that the morality, the virtue which republics require, must have its utmost link fastened to the footstool of the throne of God. May the hearts of all be open to this great truth! When WASHINGTON becomes a preacher, who will not listen?

O! ye who love your country, and labour for the preservation of her liberties; ye too, who, surrendering yourselves to your passions, have sacrificed your judgments to your zeal, come to this pure fountain of reason; it will quench your animosities: look into it as it flows; it will be a mirror to show you the path to public good; it will reflect the bright image of that eternal justice which ought to rule the universe. Yes, fellow-citizens, it is by the observance of principles contained in this last address that the happiness of the people, in these states, under the auspices of liberty, will be complete; and *that* free Constitution, the work of their own hands, will be so sacredly maintained and preserved (I use the words of WASHINGTON), as will acquire to them the glory of recommending it to the applause, the affection, and the adoption of every nation which is yet a stranger to it.

WASHINGTON retired; but he carried along with him the sentiments which a dutiful citizen ever owes to his country. Impending dangers, during this retirement, alarmed America. WASHINGTON was again ready to protect her with his shield, and, old as he was, to lead her armies to the field of battle.

III. But, that we may do justice to WASHINGTON, as a sage and a truly good man, we must view him also in private life. "When man is placed upon an elevated theatre, the eyes of the world, the glory of success, give to his soul a force and a grandeur which is often foreign to it. Pride borrows the sentiments of virtue; we do not see the person, but the personage." How many have acted as heroes at the head of armies, or appeared more than men, when conscious that they attracted universal attention; and yet, in the shade of retirement, in their common intercourse with society, have shown that they were less than men, devoid of all that real moral worth which constitutes human excellency!

To WASHINGTON the shade of retirement was as luminous as that of the most public theatre. It was here that his soul, unbent, displayed all those virtues which are the ornament and the delight of society. Humane, charitable, wise and just, in every situation, he was always consistent, always equal to himself, always evincing that rectitude of conduct was his sovereign good. The poor found, in him, a guardian; genius a patron; the honest and the meritorious a friend; the dissolute, the impious, and the profane, always an enemy. Sincerely religious, his attendance upon the service of his God was the dictate of real piety. *Such his modesty, that whilst he was the admiration of all, he alone, like Moses, descended from the mount, seemed ignorant of the light which shone around him.* Such his prudence, that not a word, not an action escaped him, which would not admit of a rational justification. This singular character of reason accompanied him through life.

Yes, brethren, it was in WASHINGTON that those four cardinal virtues, justice, prudence, temperance and fortitude, formed an union so rare and so complete. To these virtues was added an understanding the most clear and extensive. His various official communications, his addresses to his countrymen, his answers to the innumerable congratulations which he received, all of which are sufficient to form volumes; whatever came from his pen, whilst it was always distinguished by a style the most perspicuous, the most strong and manly, evinced, at the same time, a vast mind, a superior intellect, which could grasp every thing, and which laboured incessantly to promote public and private felicity.

Such was, in part, the illustrious citizen who filled so wide and honourable a space in the eye of America, and of the civilized world; and whose loss a nation this day deplores. I know that my attempts to do justice to his character have fallen infinitely short of what your affection demanded: but I am little conversant in the language of panegyric. "Recorded honours shall

59

gather round the monument of WASHINGTON, and thicken over him. It is a solid fabric, and will support the laurels that adorn it."

But ah! great and good as he was, the scene of mortal existence is closed for ever. Yes, fellow-citizens, your beloved WASHINGTON has finished his course. He is gone to appear before that God in whom he trusted; and his works have followed him. Happy moment for thee, illustrious shade! but afflictive to a nation which mourns thy loss, and which can find its consolation only in the remembrance of thy virtues, in an humble resignation to the decrees of an all-wise Providence, and in its gratitude for benefits received through thy instrumentality!

Long shall thy name be dear to thy country. Long shall the aged father, calling to his son, point to thy tomb, and bid him remember WASHINGTON! bid him recollect thy virtues, and seize the patriotic flame which once glowed within thy bosom. The tender mother, too, hanging over her beloved son, shall drop the anxious tear, and hail the name of WASHINGTON! shall exclaim, O! like him be thou brave, prudent, temperate, and just! O! be thou, like him, thy country's shield in war, its ornament in peace. And thou, America! incumbent as thou now art over the tomb of thy beloved citizen, mayest thou annually retrace his virtues, and consecrate his memory! May his actions be ever the objects of thy emulation and thy praise!

Ah! fellow-citizens, remember that virtue only is estimable in the eyes of God; and that, without it, republics are victims destined for the altars of ambition. Remember, that without just sentiments of religion, virtue perishes; a dreadful prostration of morals inevitably ensues, and, with that prostration, liberty is gone for ever. Would you shoot an arrow at the rapid lightning as it flies athwart the sky? or would you attempt to arrest the

The Apotheosis of George Washington.

ocean's tide by a single pebble? As well might you attempt to retain virtue, the basis of private and public happiness, the rock of all rational government, without religion.

Ah! in an age when religion has become the sport of libertinism and of philosophists; in an age when impiety is too often considered as the first proof of brilliancy of genius; in an age when thy religion, blessed Jesus! is scoffed and reviled by those who are ignorant of it; in an age when even our relation to a God has been derided by wickedness and folly; in such an age, religion feels more than a momentary consolation in embracing the tomb of WASHINGTON and in holding him forth as another immortal example, that man, in his greatest perfection, is ever religious and faithful.

O! ye who love your country; ye who would preserve, for yourselves and your posterity, republicanism pure and uncontaminated, again I entreat you, be it yours to cherish religion, and to bear in mind the example of WASHINGTON. Ye who yet contemn the degrading idea, that death is an eternal sleep; ye who do not rest upon the miserable and the dreadful hope of that destruction, that extinction of being, at the thought of which virtue trembles, and the soul shrinks back with horror; ye who can look beyond the grave, and there behold regions enlightened by the eternal meridian of God's unclouded smile; regions in which piety and innocence live immortal; O! make that God your friend. Then, like your beloved fellow-citizen, will you be strong in virtue, and incapable of dismay: then will you, in that awful moment which must soon tear us from all the soul holds dear in this world, be enabled, like him, to exclaim, "I have fought a good fight, I have finished my course, I have kept the faith: henceforth there is laid up for me a crown of righteousness, which the Lord, the righteous Judge, shall give me at that day; and not to me only, but unto all them that love his appearing." AMEN.

LIST OF ILLUSTRATIONS

Cover, Mount Vernon Ladies' Association.

Back cover, "Old Bruton Church, Virginia," by A. Wordsworth Thompson, The Metropolitan Museum of Art, Gift of Mrs. A. Wordsworth Thompson, 1899 (99.28), photograph copyright 1983, The Metropolitan Museum of Art.

Page 6 and 12, Mount Vernon Ladies' Association.

Page 15, Swem Library, College of William and Mary.

Page 17, Mount Vernon Ladies' Association.

Page 19, Colonial Williamsburg Foundation.

Page 30, Swem Library, College of William and Mary.

Page 32, Mount Vernon Ladies' Association.

Page 34, Library of Congress.

Page 37, Washington & Lee University.

Page 39 and 43, Mount Vernon Ladies' Association.

Page 51, Colonial Williamsburg Foundation.

Page 54 and 56, Mount Vernon Ladies' Association.

Page 61, Mount Vernon Ladies' Association, Gift of Mr. Stanley Deforest Scott.

Decorative illustrations throughout are from the Jackson Collection of eulogies, Mount Vernon Ladies' Association.